Sep 21

SPACE CAT EXPLORES STEM

What Makes a Building Strong?

by Jacqueline A. Ball
illustrations by Ken Bowser

RED
CHAIR
·PRESS·

Please visit our website at **www.redchairpress.com** for more
high-quality products for young readers.

About the Author

Jacqueline A. Ball is a Seattle-based writer, editor, and the
former publisher of Scientific American Books for Kids and Weekly
Reader Juvenile Book Clubs. Awards and honors include Booklist
Top 10 Youth Series Nonfiction (ALA), Children's Choice and Parents'
Choice Honors.

Publisher's Cataloging-In-Publication Data
Names: Ball, Jacqueline A. | Bowser, Ken, illustrator.
Title: What makes a building strong? / by Jacqueline A. Ball ; illustrations by Ken Bowser.

Description: South Egremont, MA : Red Chair Press, [2017] | Series: Space Cat explores STEM
    | Interest age level: 006-009. | Aligned to: Next Generation SCIENCE Standards. | Includes
    glossary, Did You Know sidebars and Try It! feature. | Includes bibliographical references
    and index. | Summary: "People use creative or inventive thinking to adapt the natural
    world to help them meet their needs or wants. All people use tools and technology in
    their life and jobs to solve problems. Space Cat is curious about how tools, technology and
    engineering are used to keep buildings and structures from falling down."--Provided by
    publisher.

Identifiers: LCCN 2016954287 | ISBN 978-1-63440-197-5 (library hardcover) |
    ISBN 978-1-63440-201-9 (paperback) | ISBN 978-1-63440-205-7 (ebook)

Subjects: LCSH: Structural engineering--Juvenile literature. | Buildings--Juvenile literature. |
    Technology--Juvenile literature. | CYAC: Structural engineering. | Buildings. | Technology.

Classification: LCC TA634 .B35 2017 (print) | LCC TA634 (ebook) | DDC 624.1--dc23

Photo Credits: ingimage: 5, 10, 12, 17, 19, 20, 21, 24 Shutterstock, Inc: Cover, 1, 5, 6, 7, 8, 9, 11, 13,
14, 15, 16, 17, 19, 20, 22, 23

Space Cat Explores STEM first published by:
Red Chair Press LLC   PO Box 333   South Egremont, MA 01258-0333

Printed in the United States of America
0517 1P CGBF17

Have you ever made a sandcastle at the beach? A sandcastle is a kind of **structure** [STRUCK-sher]. **Buildings** are structures where people live, work, and do all kinds of other activities.

Sandcastles are **temporary** structures. Waves wash them away quickly. Buildings are **permanent** structures. **Engineers** plan them carefully to last a long, long time. Bridges, towers, dams, and tunnels are permanent structures too.

Come along with Space Cat and her friend Dog to discover the secrets of amazing buildings and structures.

Look for important new words in **bold** letters.

Buildings and structures come in many different shapes and sizes, but each one is an important part of the world humans made. Each one is a place for people to do some important activity, such as going to school, buying groceries, driving across a river, or seeing a doctor. Without buildings and structures, modern life would not be possible.

Try It!

Space Cat:
How many different kinds of buildings and structures can you think of? Make a list. Think about how they are different from each other.

Dog:
Don't forget to list shelters for your animals!

Do you think a cave is a safe place to sleep?

Thousands of years ago, there were no human-made structures. People roamed from place to place, hunting animals and gathering plants to eat. They slept in caves.

Then humans learned to build **shelters** from tree branches. Over time, they made their shelters stronger by using mud. The mud hardened when it dried to make shelters permanent. Now people could stop roaming and settle down.

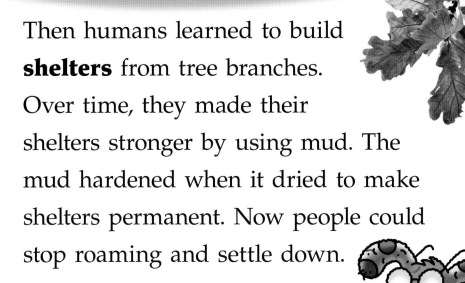

Did You Know?

Space Cat:
Most buildings and structures today are made of wood, steel, brick or stone. **Scientists** are inventing more ways to use building materials made from recycled products to help save the environment.

Today engineers and **architects** [ARK-ih-tex] make **sketches** and then draw design plans before they begin to build. The plans show careful measurements of every part of the structure, inside and out.

Did You Know?

Space Cat:
Concrete is a really old building material. Engineers in ancient Egypt used a kind of concrete to build the Pyramids.

Dog:
The foundation for my house is a concrete **slab**. It stays nice and cool in the summer and dry in the winter.

After builders figure out where to place the structure on the **site**, they dig a hole for the **foundation**. Most foundations are made of **concrete**.

The Burj Khalifa is in Dubai.

Tall structures need deep foundations. The foundation of the Burj Khalifa [BERJ kuh-LEE-fa] Tower, the tallest building in the world, goes down half a mile!

A deep, strong foundation supports the heavy weight of the building. Without that support, **gravity** could pull the building down or make it twist and topple over like a tower of blocks.

Try it!

A deep foundation lowers a structure's center of gravity. That's the place on an object or a body where its entire weight is balanced.

Your center of gravity is around your middle. See how lowering it changes your balance. Stand up and lean over slowly. How far can you lean before you start to wobble? Now sit in a chair and try the same thing. How far can you lean now?

The builders of the famous Leaning Tower of Pisa in Italy didn't set out to make the tower tilt. The problem was the muddy soil they built it on. It was too soft to support the structure. The tower started leaning before construction was completed.

Over the years engineers tried different solutions to straighten the tower, but nothing really worked. In 1990, a team of scientists made a plan to steady the tower by pulling it with cables attached to a concrete base. Success! They were able to reduce the amount of tilt enough to keep the tower stable. It could stay standing for hundreds more years now.

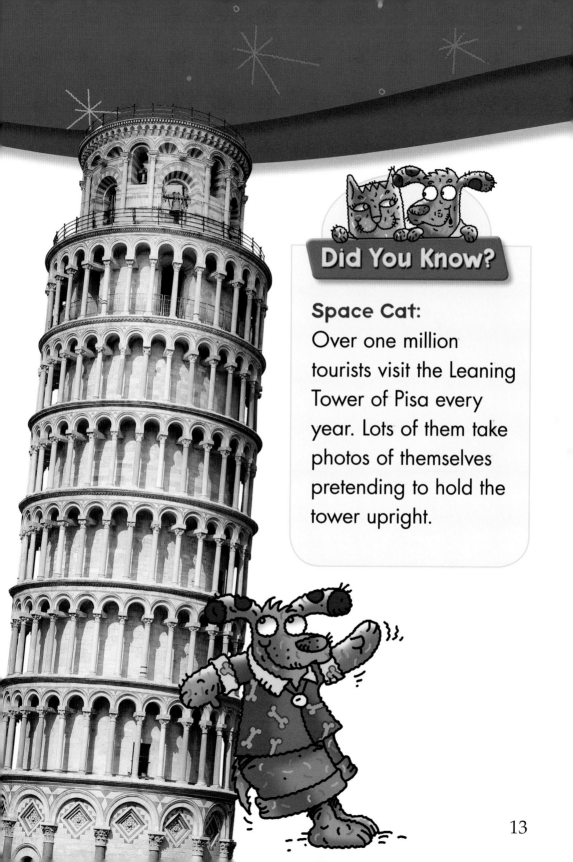

Did You Know?

Space Cat:
Over one million tourists visit the Leaning Tower of Pisa every year. Lots of them take photos of themselves pretending to hold the tower upright.

A structure's **frame** is attached to its foundation. The frame spreads out the building's weight so there's not too much in any one place. It holds up the walls and roof like your **skeleton** holds up your body.

Most houses have wooden frames. **Skyscrapers** have frames made of the strongest steel.

Did You Know?

Space Cat:
Tightrope walkers spread their weight for better balance by holding a **horizontal** bar.

In some places, buildings must stand up to **earthquakes** as well as gravity. Engineers today use special building materials and **techniques** to create earthquake-proof buildings.

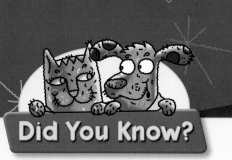

Engineers long ago designed earthquake-proof buildings too. For the buildings at Machu Picchu [MAH-choo PEA-choo] in Peru, the Incan people constructed walls using stones of different shapes and sizes. They arranged the stones so they fit together tightly, like Lego™ or jigsaw puzzle pieces. Machu Picchu has stayed standing for 500 years.

Of course, buildings need
to do much more than just stand up
straight! They need to work well for
the people who use them. People need
to get in and out quickly. They need
to stay comfortable and move around
safely inside.

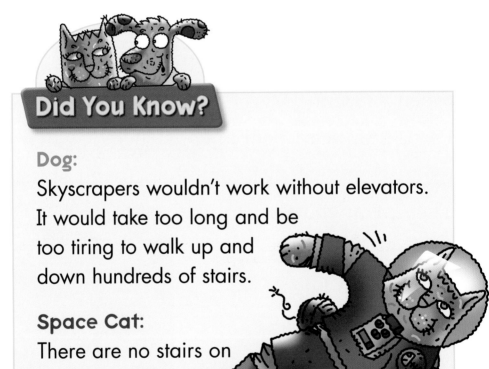

Did You Know?

Dog:
Skyscrapers wouldn't work without elevators.
It would take too long and be
too tiring to walk up and
down hundreds of stairs.

Space Cat:
There are no stairs on
a space walk!

Toronto's CN Tower rises over the city.

In tall buildings, **revolving doors** let crowds of people enter and exit one at a time. Elevators carry workers and visitors from one floor to another in seconds. Outdoor glass-fronted elevators give riders a view of the whole city. The tallest one in the world is at the CN Tower in Toronto, Canada.

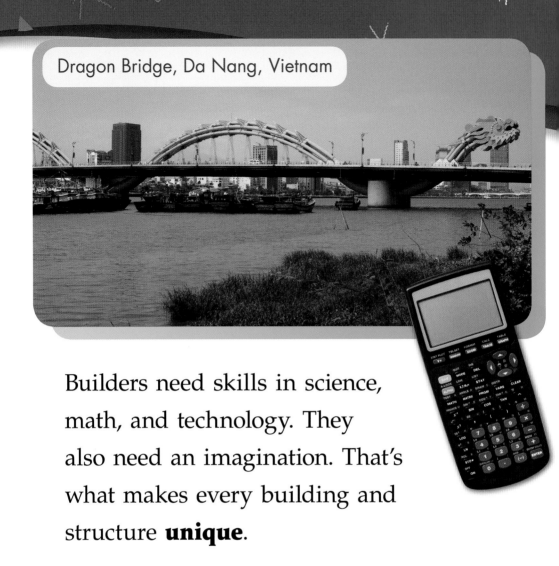

Dragon Bridge, Da Nang, Vietnam

Builders need skills in science, math, and technology. They also need an imagination. That's what makes every building and structure **unique**.

One of the most unique structures in the world is the Dragon Bridge in Da Nang, Vietnam. It has a cement dragon with fire coming out of its mouth! The fire comes from a gas flame. Thousands of colored lights make the dragon glow at night.

Try it!

Space Cat:

Use your imagination to dream up a special structure. Think about what it would be used for. What materials would you choose? How would you paint it or decorate it to make it unique? Write down some ideas and make a sketch, then a design plan.

Dog:

Brainstorm with friends for more ideas and more fun!

Glossary

3D printer Machine that makes three-dimensional objects by putting layers of material on top of each other

Architect Person who designs buildings

Building Structure used by people to do activities

Concrete Hard mixture of broken rocks, water, and other materials

Earthquake The shaking of a part of Earth's surface

Engineer Person who plans and makes equipment, machines, and buildings

Foundation Strong base that supports a structure

Frame Arrangement of parts that support the shape of something

Gravity A pulling force of nature

Horizontal Going from left to right in a flat line, like the horizon

Permanent Lasting a very long time

Revolving door Door with individual sections that turns as it is pushed

Scientist Person who studies the natural world

Shelter Structure that protects people

Site Spot where a building will go up

Skeleton Frame of bones that supports a human body

Sketch Quick drawing

Skyscraper Very tall building in a city

Slab Thick, flat piece of concrete or other hard material

Structure Something built from different parts and designed to stand on its own

Technique Special way of doing something

Technology Use of science to invent things or solve problems

Temporary Lasting only a short time

Unique One of a kind

Learn More in the Library

Books

Armstrong, Simon. *Cool Architecture: 50 Fantastic Facts for Kids of All Ages.* Pavilion Books, 2015.

Latham, Donna. Skyscrapers: *Investigate Feats of Engineering.* White River Press, 2013.

Web Sites

PBS: Building Big
pbs.org/wgbh/buildingbig/

TIME for Kids: How 3D Printers Work
timeforkids.com/photos-video/video/
how-3d-printers-work-203276

index